S'more Tips

- Spritz the spoon, rubber scraper, and measuring cups with cooking spray before measuring marshmallow creme so it releases cleanly.

- Coat a pizza cutter with oil or cooking spray to cut through sticky marshmallow-laden desserts more easily.

- For clean straight cuts on cold bars and desserts, dip a sharp knife in hot water and wipe clean after each cut.

- To crush graham crackers with less mess, place them in a heavy-duty zippered plastic bag; seal bag and crush crackers with a rolling pin. Measure out whatever you need and keep the remainder for use in another recipe.

- When toasting marshmallows under a hot broiler, watch carefully to prevent overbrowning.

Printed in the United States of America
by G&R Publishing Co.

Distributed By:

507 Industrial Street
Waverly, IA 50677

ISBN 978-1-56383-493-6
Item #7089

graham crackers + melty chocolate + toasty marshmallows = s'mores to love!

Pick your favorite combos to move beyond traditional s'mores.

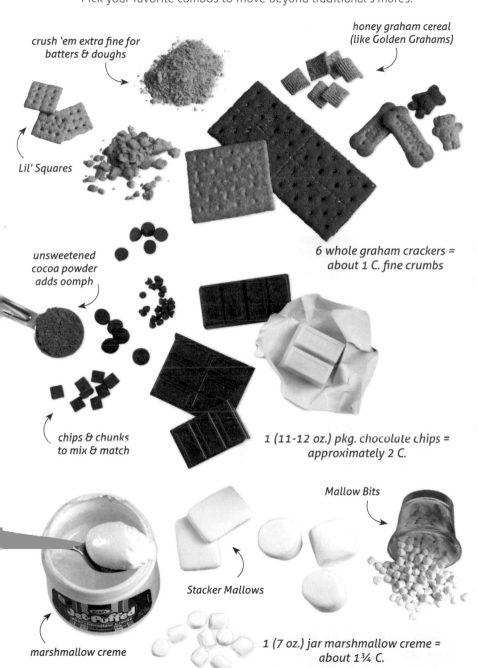

crush 'em extra fine for batters & doughs

honey graham cereal (like Golden Grahams)

Lil' Squares

unsweetened cocoa powder adds oomph

6 whole graham crackers = about 1 C. fine crumbs

chips & chunks to mix & match

1 (11-12 oz.) pkg. chocolate chips = approximately 2 C.

Mallow Bits

Stacker Mallows

marshmallow creme

1 (7 oz.) jar marshmallow creme = about 1¾ C.

serves 12

S'BERRY ICE CREAM S'MOREWICHES

you'll need

8 oz. semi-sweet baking chocolate

6 T. butter

5 T. flour, sifted

2 T. chocolate graham cracker crumbs

3 eggs

1 C. brown sugar

¼ tsp. salt

½ tsp. vanilla

4 to 5 C. strawberry ice cream

½ C. chopped fresh strawberries

⅓ C. Mallow Bits

to make

Heat oven to 350°. Line two 9 x 13˝ baking pans with parchment paper and coat with cooking spray. Chop the chocolate. Melt butter and stir in chocolate until smooth; let cool.

Combine flour and crumbs. In another bowl, beat eggs, brown sugar, salt, and vanilla on high speed for 8 to 10 minutes, until mixture falls from beaters in a wide ribbon. Stir in cooled chocolate. Fold in flour mixture. Spread half the batter *(about 1¾ cups)* in each pan. Bake 8 to 11 minutes or until brownies test done. Cool to room temperature and then flip brownies out onto cooling racks. Remove paper and chill.

Line a clean 9 x 13˝ pan with plastic wrap, leaving a generous overhang. Set one brownie layer into lined pan, top side down. Soften ice cream just until spreadable; stir in strawberries and Mallow Bits. Spread ice cream over brownie in pan. Set remaining brownie on ice cream, top side up; press gently to make level. Cover and freeze overnight.

Lift plastic to remove dessert from pan. Slice into "sandwiches" and wrap individually. Return to freezer until needed.

Deep Dish Cookies

makes 20

you'll need

- 8 milk chocolate candy bars, divided
- 1 C. butter, softened
- 1½ C. brown sugar
- 2 eggs
- 2 tsp. vanilla
- 1½ C. graham cracker crumbs
- 1 tsp. baking soda
- 1 tsp. salt
- 2¼ C. flour
- 1 C. Mallow Bits
- Regular marshmallows

Heat oven to 350°. Coat jumbo muffin cups with cooking spray. Coarsely chop six candy bars and set aside.

Beat butter and brown sugar until light and fluffy. Beat in eggs and vanilla. Add crumbs, baking soda, salt, and flour; mix well. Stir in Mallow Bits and chopped chocolate. Press ⅓ cup cookie dough into each muffin cup. Bake 23 to 26 minutes or until golden brown.

Remove from oven and press a marshmallow into each cookie. Change oven to broil setting and place pan under a hot broiler to toast marshmallows. Remove from oven and let cool 3 minutes; press a candy bar segment into each marshmallow. Let cool in pan for 10 minutes; run a knife around edge of cups to remove cookies. Cool completely.

Nutty Crumb Crispies

makes 16

you'll need

- 3 T. sugar
- 3 T. brown sugar
- 6 T. graham cracker crumbs
- 3 T. cold butter, cut into pieces
- 1 (8 oz.) tube refrigerated crescent rolls
- 1 C. mini marshmallows
- ¼ C. mini chocolate chips
- ¼ C. chopped pecans

Heat oven to 400°. Combine sugar, brown sugar, and crumbs in a bowl. Cut in butter until crumbly.

Line a cookie sheet with parchment paper. Separate crescent roll dough into eight triangles and place on cookie sheet; pat dough to enlarge triangles slightly. Sprinkle crumb mixture evenly over each triangle and press in place. Sprinkle with marshmallows, chocolate chips, and pecans; press gently. Bake 8 minutes or until golden.

Let cool before cutting in half to make smaller triangles. Drizzle with Marshmallow Glaze.

Marshmallow Glaze: Whisk together 1 T. softened butter, 1 T. marshmallow creme, ¾ C. powdered sugar, 1 tsp. vanilla, and about 1 T. milk until smooth.

Stuffed PB Bars

makes 16

you'll need

- ½ C. butter, softened
- ¼ C. sugar
- ½ C. brown sugar
- 1 egg
- 1 tsp. vanilla
- 1¼ C. flour
- 1 tsp. baking powder
- ¼ tsp. salt
- 1 C. graham cracker crumbs
- 16 peanut butter cups
- 1¼ C. marshmallow creme

Heat oven to 350°. Line an 8 x 8″ baking pan with parchment paper and coat with cooking spray.

Beat together butter, sugar, and brown sugar until fluffy. Beat in egg and vanilla. Stir in flour, baking powder, salt, and crumbs until blended. Spread ⅔ of dough over bottom of pan. Lightly press unwrapped peanut butter cups into dough to cover evenly. Spread marshmallow creme on top. Press remaining dough into an 8 x 8″ square on a nonstick surface and then set on top of marshmallow creme layer; press down lightly. Bake 30 minutes or until edges begin to brown. Let cool at least 2 hours before removing from pan to cut.

Crispy Mallowed Brownies

Heat oven to 350°. Mix and bake a 9 x 13" pan of fudge brownies according to package directions. Remove from oven, sprinkle with 1 (10 oz.) bag mini marshmallows, and bake 3 minutes more, until puffy and slightly melted. Cool completely.

Combine 2 C. semi-sweet chocolate chips, 1 C. creamy peanut butter and 1 T. butter in a saucepan; cook and stir over low heat until melted. Remove from heat and stir in 1 C. crisp rice cereal and ½ C. crushed Teddy Grahams. Spread over brownies and chill until firm.

makes 25

S'more Chow

Melt 1¾ C. mixture of semi-sweet and milk chocolate chips in the microwave, stirring until smooth. Stir in ½ C. hazelnut spread *(like Nutella)*. Pour over 6 C. honey graham cereal and stir until coated. Stir in 2 C. mini marshmallows, ½ C. semi-sweet chocolate chips, and ½ C. whole almonds. Transfer to a large resealable container and sprinkle with 1½ C. powdered sugar. Seal and shake until everything is coated in white.

serves 12

9

Fudgy S'mores Squares

makes 25 squares

you'll need

- 2 C. graham cracker crumbs
- ½ C. butter, melted
- 1 C. sugar, divided
- ¾ tsp. salt, divided
- 2 C. semi-sweet chocolate chips
- 1 (14 oz.) can sweetened condensed milk
- ½ C. light corn syrup
- 2 egg whites
- ¼ tsp. cream of tartar
- 1½ tsp. vanilla

Heat oven to 350°. Line a 9 x 9″ baking pan with foil. In a bowl, mix crumbs, butter, ¼ cup sugar and ½ teaspoon salt; press evenly into pan. Bake 10 minutes and set crust aside.

Combine chocolate chips and sweetened condensed milk in a saucepan over medium-low heat; stir until melted. Pour over crust. In another saucepan, combine ¼ cup water, remaining ¾ cup sugar, corn syrup, and remaining ¼ teaspoon salt. Bring to a boil over medium-high heat and cook until a candy thermometer reads 240°. Remove from heat.

In a clean bowl, beat egg whites and cream of tartar on medium speed to soft peaks. Drizzle warm syrup into bowl and beat into egg whites. Increase mixer speed and beat 7 to 8 minutes, until thick and glossy. Beat in vanilla. Spread over chocolate layer. Set pan under a hot broiler until fluff layer is lightly browned. Cool completely.

Frozen Banana Pops

makes 8

you'll need

- 4 bananas
- 1 C. semi sweet chocolate chips
- ½ tsp. canola oil
- ¼ C. coarse graham cracker crumbs
- ¼ C. Mallow Bits, coarsely crushed

Peel bananas and cut in half crosswise. Insert a popsicle stick about halfway into each cut end and freeze on a foil-lined cookie sheet for 20 minutes.

Microwave chocolate chips with oil at 50% power until melted and smooth, stirring several times.

Place crumbs and Mallow Bits on separate plates. Pour chocolate mixture into a heatproof bowl and set over a pot of simmering water to keep warm. One at a time, coat frozen bananas with chocolate and quickly sprinkle with crumbs and Mallow Bits. Return to cookie sheet. Freeze coated bananas at least 30 minutes; thaw slightly before eating.

makes 12

S'MORES RASPBERRY HAND PIES

you'll need

2 oz. cream cheese, softened

1 C. marshmallow creme

½ C. sugar, divided

½ C. mini chocolate chips

1 (14.1 oz.) pkg. refrigerated pie crusts (2 ct.)

½ C. graham cracker crumbs

3 T. butter, melted

1 C. fresh raspberries, halved

to make

Heat oven to 425°. Line a cookie sheet with parchment paper. Mix cream cheese with marshmallow creme, ¼ cup sugar, and chocolate chips; set filling aside.

Unroll pie crusts on a floured surface. With a 5˝ cookie cutter, cut six rounds from each crust, rerolling scraps as needed. Mix crumbs and remaining ¼ cup sugar. Brush one side of each crust with butter and coat with crumbs; reserve remaining crumbs. Set rounds on cookie sheet, crumb side down. Spoon 1 tablespoon filling onto half of each round, leaving edges bare. Set a few raspberry halves on filling. Sprinkle with 1 teaspoon reserved crumbs. Moisten crust edges with water and fold crust over filling. Crimp edges together with a fork. Bake 11 to 12 minutes or until golden brown. Let cool and drizzle with icing.

Icing: Whisk 1 C. sifted powdered sugar with enough warm water to make a drizzling consistency.

13

oven

makes 20

CRUNCHY S'MORES BISCOTTI

you'll need

1 C. flour

½ C. unsweetened cocoa powder

½ C. graham cracker crumbs

⅓ C. sugar

¾ tsp. baking powder

¼ tsp. salt

¼ C. butter, melted

1 C. marshmallow creme

1 egg

½ tsp. vanilla

¾ C. milk chocolate chips

3 squares white almond bark

Coarse graham cracker crumbs

Heat oven to **375°**. Line a cookie sheet with parchment paper.

Whisk together first six ingredients and set aside. In another bowl, beat butter, marshmallow creme, egg, and vanilla until well blended. Add flour mixture and mix until stiff dough forms. Stir in chocolate chips. Divide dough in half on cookie sheet and shape into 5″ logs; flatten slightly. Bake 20 to 25 minutes or until firm. Let cool 30 minutes. Cut logs into ¾″ slices with a serrated knife.

Reduce oven temperature to 325°. Arrange slices on cookie sheet (cut side down) and bake again for 10 minutes. Flip and bake 8 minutes more or until dry. Cool completely.

Melt almond bark in the microwave until smooth. Dip one end of biscotti into bark and let excess drip off. Sprinkle with coarse crumbs and set on parchment paper to dry.

Raspberry Cream

Twist open a Berry Burst Ice Cream Oreo cookie and layer one cookie half with a toasted pink marshmallow and fresh raspberries. Top with the other cookie half.

Chocolate Cherry Goodness

Between chocolate graham crackers, tuck some cherry pie filling, chocolate candy squares, and a toasted marshmallow. Yum!

Berry Delish

Set pieces of Cookies 'n' Creme candy bar, a toasted marshmallow, and fresh blackberries between two chocolate graham crackers.

Jazzed-Up Cookie Crunch

On an oatmeal cookie, layer sliced strawberries, dark chocolate chips, and a toasted pink marshmallow. Top with another cookie.

Double Mint Delight

Twist open a Mint Oreo cookie. Place a toasted marshmallow and Andes mint wafer between the cookie halves. Delightful!

Blonde Beauties

makes 15

you'll need

- 1½ C. flour
- 1 C. graham cracker crumbs
- ½ tsp. baking powder
- ¼ tsp. salt
- 1 C. butter, melted and cooled
- 1½ C. brown sugar
- 1 tsp. vanilla
- 2 eggs
- 1 (7 oz.) pkg. chocolate stars, chopped
- 2 C. mini marshmallows

Heat oven to 350°. Coat a 9 x 13″ baking pan with cooking spray.

Stir together first four ingredients. In a large bowl, beat butter and brown sugar on medium speed until creamy. Beat in vanilla and eggs. Gradually beat in flour mixture. Spread batter in pan and bake 23 to 25 minutes or until golden brown around edges.

Remove from oven and sprinkle with chopped chocolate and marshmallows; return to oven and bake 10 minutes more or until marshmallows are puffy and golden brown. Let cool in pan at least 10 minutes before cutting.

Gooey S'mores Pie

serves 10

you'll need

- ½ C. butter, softened
- ½ C. sugar
- 1 egg
- 1 tsp. vanilla
- 1 C. flour
- 1 tsp. baking powder
- 1 C. graham cracker crumbs
- 1 (7 oz.) jar marshmallow creme
- 3 (1.55 oz.) milk chocolate candy bars
- 1 C. mini marshmallows
- ½ C. chopped pecans
- Mini chocolate chips

Heat oven to 350°. Coat a 9″ pie plate with cooking spray.

Beat butter and sugar until creamy. Beat in egg and vanilla. Add flour, baking powder, and crumbs; mix well. With buttered fingers, press half of dough over bottom and up sides of pie plate. Spread marshmallow creme over crust. Break candy bars and arrange pieces on top. Sprinkle with marshmallows and pecans.

Pat remaining dough into flat pieces and place randomly over filling, allowing some to peek through. Pinch dough edges together around rim. Bake 20 to 22 minutes or until lightly browned. Sprinkle chocolate chips on top and bake 2 minutes more. Cool completely before slicing.

serves 2

ÜBER GOURMET
HOT COCOA

you'll need

Regular marshmallows

3 T. graham cracker crumbs

3 C. milk

¼ C. unsweetened cocoa powder

Chocolate syrup

3 to 4 T. sugar

Pinch of salt

to make

Rub a marshmallow around the rim of two oven-safe mugs to moisten. Dip rims in crumbs to coat and set aside to dry.

Heat milk over medium-low heat until hot, but not scalding. Whisk in cocoa powder, 2 tablespoons chocolate syrup, sugar, and salt until well blended; heat 1 minute more. Pour into prepared mugs. Cut a few marshmallows into thirds and top each mug with marshmallow pieces. Set mugs on a baking sheet and place under a hot broiler briefly to brown marshmallows. Remove and drizzle with more chocolate syrup. Serve promptly.

21

S'mores Pretzel Pizza

serves 14

you'll need

1 (16.5 oz.) roll refrigerated chocolate chip cookie dough, softened

2½ C. mini marshmallows

¾ to 1 C. coarsely broken graham crackers

½ C. milk chocolate chips

25 mini pretzel twists, broken

Heat oven to 350°. Line a 12″ to 14″ pizza pan with parchment paper and coat with cooking spray. Press dough evenly into bottom of pan. Bake 8 minutes or until center is set and edges begin to brown.

Sprinkle marshmallows over partially baked crust, followed by crackers, chocolate chips, and pretzels. Return to oven and bake 6 to 8 minutes more or until marshmallows are puffy and lightly browned. Cool slightly before slicing with a greased pizza cutter. Eat while warm and gooey or let cool completely.

No-Bake Crunch Bars

Coat an 8 x 8" baking pan with cooking spray. Microwave ½ C. butter, 1 C. milk chocolate chips, and 1 C. semi-sweet chocolate chips; stir until smooth and glossy. Stir in ¼ C. light corn syrup.

Reserve ½ C. chocolate mixture for later use. To remaining chocolate mixture, stir in 1¾ C. coarsely crushed graham crackers and 2 C. mini marshmallows. Press mixture into pan. Pour reserved chocolate over bars. Cover and chill at least 2 hours before cutting.

makes 16

Bits & Chips Cheeseball

Beat 1 (8 oz.) package softened cream cheese with ½ C. softened butter. Stir in ¾ C. powdered sugar, 2 T. brown sugar, ¼ tsp. vanilla, ½ C. mini chocolate chips, and ½ C. chocolate Mallow Bits. Cover and chill for 2 hours.

Shape mixture into a ball; wrap and chill for 1 hour. Roll cheeseball in a mixture of ½ C. graham cracker crumbs, 1 T. brown sugar, and 2 T. chopped pecans. Serve with chocolate or regular graham crackers or sliced apples.

serves 30

Chocolate-Butterscotch Cookies

makes 42

you'll need

1 C. butter, softened

½ C. sugar

½ C. brown sugar

2 eggs

1 T. vanilla

2 C. flour

¼ C. graham cracker crumbs

2 T. unsweetened cocoa powder

1 tsp. baking soda

½ tsp. salt

1 (3.9 oz.) pkg. chocolate instant pudding mix

2 C. butterscotch chips

¾ to 1 C. Mallow Bits

Heat oven to 350°. Line cookie sheets with parchment paper.

Beat together butter, sugar, and brown sugar until light and fluffy. Beat in eggs and vanilla. In another bowl, combine flour, crumbs, cocoa powder, baking soda, and salt. Add to butter mixture and mix well. Beat in pudding mix. Stir in butterscotch chips and Mallow Bits.

Drop by heaping tablespoonful onto cookie sheets and bake 11 to 13 minutes or until cooked through. Let cool on pan for 10 minutes before removing to cooling rack to cool completely.

White Chocolate Cake Bars

makes 16

you'll need

1 (15.25 oz.) box
   yellow cake mix

1 egg

½ C. butter, softened

4½ whole graham crackers

2 C. white baking chips

2 C. mini marshmallows

½ C. sweetened
   condensed milk

Heat oven to 350°. Line an 8 x 8″ baking pan with foil, extending it beyond pan edges; coat with cooking spray.

Stir together cake mix, egg, and butter with large spoon until dough forms and then work it with hands to shape dough into a ball. Divide dough in half and press one half into bottom of pan. Arrange crackers over dough. Sprinkle baking chips and marshmallows on top.

Flatten pieces of remaining dough and arrange over marshmallows until mostly covered *(some filling may peek through)*. Drizzle with sweetened condensed milk. Bake 28 to 33 minutes or until golden brown. Let cool 5 minutes before loosening edges with a plastic knife. Cool completely. Lift foil and bars from pan; peel off foil before cutting.

Half-Pint Mallow Dip

Combine ½ C. mini marshmallows and 1 T. milk chocolate chips in a small microwave-safe bowl. Microwave until chocolate melts and marshmallows are puffy. Stir together lightly and serve right away with graham cracker sticks or apple slices.

serves 1

Caramel Grahams

Heat oven to 350°. Line a 10 x 15" rimmed baking sheet with foil. Arrange 12 whole graham crackers over foil and cover with 2 C. mini marshmallows.

Combine ¾ C. butter and ¾ C. brown sugar in a saucepan over medium heat. Cook and stir until sugar dissolves. Remove from heat and stir in 1 tsp. vanilla; drizzle over marshmallows. Sprinkle with 1 C. milk chocolate chips, 1 C. sliced almonds, and ½ C. coconut. Bake 14 to 16 minutes or until browned. Cool completely. Cut into 2" squares and then diagonally into triangles.

makes 72 pieces

Caramel Corn Crunch

Toss together 6 oz. caramel popcorn, ¾ C. mixed nuts, 2¼ C. honey graham cereal, 1 C. peanut M&Ms, and 1 C. mini marshmallows; spread on a large rimmed baking sheet.

Melt three or four squares chocolate almond bark and drizzle over popcorn mixture; let dry. Melt two squares white almond bark and drizzle again; let dry. Break apart for nibbling.

serves 16

S'more the Merrier Dip

Microwave 1½ C. dark chocolate chips and 1 (14 oz.) can sweetened condensed milk until melted and smooth, stirring often. Pour mixture into a microwave-safe pie plate and drop spoonfuls of marshmallow creme *(about ½ C.)* over chocolate. Microwave for 30 seconds and swirl together with a knife. Serve with graham crackers, pretzels, peanut butter cookies, or fresh fruit slices.

serves 12

makes 12

COCO MALLOW
SHORT STACK

you'll need

½ C. flour

½ C. whole wheat flour

2 tsp. baking powder

2 T. unsweetened cocoa powder

2 T. brown sugar

½ tsp. salt

¾ C. milk

1 egg

3 T. sour cream

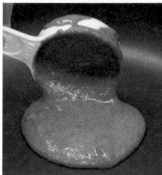

to make

Stir together first six ingredients. In another bowl, whisk together milk and egg; pour into flour mixture and stir until just combined. Fold in sour cream.

Heat a nonstick griddle or large skillet over medium heat. For each pancake, pour about ¼ cup batter onto hot griddle and cook until bubbles form around edges, about 2 minutes. Flip and cook 1 to 2 minutes more. Drizzle pancakes with Marshmallow Sauce. Top with fresh berries, if desired.

Marshmallow Sauce: Whisk together 1 C. marshmallow creme and 1½ T. boiling water until blended.

29

Sweet & Easy Popcorn Balls

makes 12

you'll need

- 2 C. milk chocolate chips, divided
- 9 C. popped popcorn
- 1 C. broken honey graham cereal
- 3 T. butter
- 1 (7 oz.) jar marshmallow creme
- 1 tsp. vanilla
- 1 T. shortening
- 2 squares white almond bark, optional

Chill 1 cup chocolate chips. Combine popcorn and cereal in a large bowl and set aside.

Melt butter in a nonstick saucepan over medium heat. Stir in marshmallow creme until melted and smooth. Remove from heat and stir in vanilla. Pour marshmallow mixture over popcorn and cereal; stir until well coated. Quickly stir in cold chocolate chips. With buttered hands, form mixture into balls and set on parchment paper to cool. *(If you like, insert popsicle sticks, pressing mixture firmly around sticks.)* Reshape balls as needed while they cool.

Microwave remaining 1 cup chocolate chips and shortening until melted, stirring well. Drizzle chocolate mixture over popcorn balls and let dry. If desired, melt almond bark and drizzle lightly over popcorn balls; let dry.

Sweetly Spicy Party Mix

In a microwave-safe bowl, mix 2 C. Chocolate Chex, 2 C. Cinnamon Oatmeal Squares, and 4 C. popped popcorn. Drizzle with ¼ cup melted butter and toss well. Microwave 1 minute and stir; microwave 1 minute more and stir again.

Mix ¼ C. sugar, 1 tsp. cinnamon, and ⅛ to ¼ tsp. each cayenne pepper and salt. Sprinkle half the seasonings over cereal mixture, stir, and repeat. Microwave 1 minute and let cool. Stir in ½ C. cold milk chocolate chips and ½ C. mini marshmallows. Spread on parchment paper to cool completely.

makes 8 cups

Trail Mix to Go

In a large bowl, combine 1 (16 oz.) box honey graham cereal, 1 (16 oz.) bag mini marshmallows, 1 (11.5 oz.) pkg. milk chocolate chips, and 2 C. cashews or dry roasted peanuts. Add bits of dried fruit, if desired. Mix well. Store in an airtight container or divide among plastic sandwich bags for easy toting.

makes 16 cups

serves 12

FROSTY MOCHA ICE CREAM CAKE

you'll need

16 whole graham crackers, broken

1 C. toasted whole almonds

3 T. sugar

½ C. butter, melted

1½ (1.5 qt.) cartons coffee ice cream

2 (12.8 oz.) jars fudge sauce

1 (7 oz.) jar marshmallow creme *(or 8 oz. whipped topping)*

2 C. mini marshmallows

Marshmallows may be toasted with a culinary torch.

Heat oven to **350°**.

Combine graham crackers, almonds, and sugar in a food processor; grind well. Add butter and process until moist crumbs form. Press crumb mixture into bottom and up sides of a 9˝ springform pan. Bake about 12 minutes or until edges are golden brown. Cool completely.

Soften ice cream until spreadable. Spread 3 cups ice cream in crust *(about half of one carton)*. Spoon ¾ cup fudge sauce over ice cream. Freeze until sauce is set, about 15 minutes. Repeat with another layer of ice cream and fudge sauce; freeze until sauce is set. Spread 3 more cups ice cream on top; cover and freeze overnight.

Spread marshmallow creme over ice cream and sprinkle with marshmallows. Return to freezer for 10 minutes *(or more)*.

Before serving, wrap a warm wet towel around outside of pan for 1 minute to loosen cake. Remove side of pan before slicing. Warm up remaining fudge sauce in the microwave and drizzle over each piece.

Bacon-Caramel Crunch

Set crisp bacon strips on a chocolate graham cracker. Add a Ghiradelli Dark & Sea Salt Caramel Square and a toasted marshmallow. Top with another cracker and say "Mmmm."

Granny's Apple S'mores

Core and thinly slice an apple crosswise. Sandwich a peanut butter cup and a toasted marshmallow between two apple slices.

Nutter Butter Goodies

Twist open a Nutter Butter cookie. Set a hunk of Mr. Goodbar and a toasted marshmallow between the cookie halves.

Pleasin' Pieces

Smear chocolate frosting on one graham cracker and sprinkle with Reese's Pieces. Spread peanut butter on another cracker. Slip a toasted marshmallow between the crackers and squish together.

Banana Ritz Blitz

Spread peanut butter on a Ritz cracker and sprinkle with milk chocolate chips. Top with a toasted marshmallow, banana slices, and another cracker.

serves 16

PARTY S'MORE CHEESECAKE

you'll need

2 C. graham cracker crumbs

¼ C. sugar

7 T. butter, melted

3 (8 oz.) pkgs. cream cheese, softened

1 C. brown sugar

⅓ C. marshmallow creme

1 T. vanilla

4 eggs

2 C. milk chocolate chips, divided

¼ C. heavy cream

to make

Heat oven to 425°. Coat a 9″ springform pan with cooking spray. Mix crumbs, sugar, and butter; reserve ½ cup for topping. Press remaining crumbs over bottom of pan. Bake 5 to 6 minutes or until beginning to brown; let cool.

Beat cream cheese until creamy. Beat in brown sugar, marshmallow creme, vanilla, and eggs until smooth. Sprinkle 1 cup chocolate chips over crust. Pour filling on top. Bake 15 minutes; then reduce oven temperature to 225° and bake 45 minutes more or until lightly browned and center is set but still wiggles *(don't test doneness with a knife)*. Turn off oven. Leave cheesecake in oven with door open slightly until cheesecake has cooled to room temperature. Cover and chill at least 3 hours.

Microwave remaining 1 cup chocolate chips with cream, stirring until smooth. Spread over cheesecake and sprinkle with reserved crumbs. Cover and refrigerate at least 1 hour *(up to 4 days)*. Loosen cheesecake from pan with a warm knife and remove side of pan before slicing.

37

makes 30

7-LAYER S'MOREOS

you'll need

1½ C. pretzel crumbs

½ C. graham cracker crumbs

¼ C. brown sugar

½ C. butter, melted

1 (7 oz.) jar marshmallow creme

1 C. crunchy peanut butter

24 chocolate sandwich cookies *(such as Oreos)*

1½ C. mini M&Ms or milk chocolate chips

¾ C. sweetened condensed milk

2 C. mini marshmallows

Heat oven to **350°**. Line a 9 x 13˝ baking pan with parchment paper.

Mix pretzel and cracker crumbs with brown sugar; stir in butter. Press crumb mixture into bottom of pan. Drop marshmallow creme by spoonful over crust. Spread a spoonful of peanut butter on each cookie and arrange cookies over marshmallow creme.

Sprinkle with M&Ms. Drizzle sweetened condensed milk over everything and bake for 25 minutes. Let cool 10 minutes. Scatter marshmallows evenly over the top and set pan under a hot broiler to brown marshmallows, 20 to 30 seconds.

Cool completely and then refrigerate for 1 to 2 hours. Lift parchment paper and bars from pan. Cut with a warm sharp knife, rinsing knife often.

Bundtiful Breakfast Rolls

serves 12

you'll need

- ½ C. sugar
- ¾ C. graham cracker crumbs
- 24 frozen dinner rolls, thawed but still cold*
- 1 C. chocolate chunks
- 1 C. mini marshmallows
- ¾ C. butter
- 1½ C. marshmallow creme
- 1 tsp. vanilla

Coat a 10˝ Bundt pan with cooking spray. Mix sugar and crumbs in a bowl. Quarter each roll and coat in crumb mixture; reserve remaining crumbs.

In pan, layer ⅓ each roll pieces, chocolate chunks, and marshmallows. Sprinkle with ⅓ of remaining crumb mixture *(about ¼ cup)*. Repeat to make three layers.

Melt butter in a nonstick saucepan. Whisk in marshmallow creme until melted and boiling. Cook and stir 1 minute. Remove from heat and stir in vanilla; let cool 10 minutes. Pour over layers in pan. Cover with sprayed plastic wrap and let rise until 1˝ below top of pan.

Heat oven to 350°. Uncover pan and set on a cookie sheet. Bake 40 to 45 minutes, covering with foil the last 15 minutes to prevent overbrowning. Invert onto a serving platter and serve warm.

* Thaw in refrigerator overnight.

Company Trifle

serves 12

you'll need

- 1 (8 x 8″) pan baked brownies
- 1 (5.9 oz.) pkg. chocolate instant pudding mix
- 4 C. milk
- 4 C. torn angel food cake
- 12 whole graham crackers, coarsely broken, plus extra for topping
- 1 (8 oz.) tub whipped topping, thawed
- 1 (7 oz.) jar marshmallow creme
- 1 C. mini marshmallows*
- Chocolate candy bar

Cut brownies into ¾″ pieces. Whisk together pudding mix and milk until thick and smooth, about 2 minutes. In a trifle bowl, layer half each of the brownie and cake pieces, pudding, and crackers. Whisk together whipped topping and marshmallow creme; spread half the mixture over cracker layer.

Repeat layers, ending with whipped topping mixture. Top with marshmallows, candy bar segments, and extra broken crackers.

If desired, broil marshmallows on a greased parchment paper-lined cookie sheet until golden brown; let cool before arranging over top of dessert.

PB Surprise Cookies

makes 18

you'll need

1¾ C. flour
¾ tsp. baking soda
½ tsp. salt
½ C. butter, softened
¾ C. creamy peanut butter
½ C. sugar
½ C. brown sugar
1 egg
1 tsp. vanilla
1½ C. dark chocolate chips
Lil' Squares grahams
Mini marshmallows

Heat oven to 350°. Line cookie sheets with parchment paper.

Whisk together first three ingredients. In another bowl, beat butter, peanut butter, sugar, and brown sugar until light and fluffy. Mix in egg and vanilla. Gradually beat in flour mixture until dough forms. Stir in chocolate chips.

Form dough into 2˝ balls and flatten with fingers. Place a Lil' Square and two or three marshmallows in the center and wrap dough around to cover. Place on cookie sheets and flatten slightly. Bake 11 to 13 minutes or until golden brown on the bottom *(don't over-bake)*. Cool on pan for 5 minutes before removing to a cooling rack to cool completely.

Frozen Mint Chippers

makes 12

you'll need

- 12 whole chocolate graham crackers
- 1 C. mini chocolate chips
- 1 C. Mallow Bits
- 1 (1.5 to 1.75 qt.) rectangular carton mint chip ice cream

Break each cracker into two squares. *(For clean breaks, gently "saw" along perforation with a serrated knife before snapping cracker in two.)* Mix some of the chocolate chips and Mallow Bits in a shallow dish.

Open carton to expose block of ice cream. With a warm sharp knife, cut a 1″ crosswise slice of ice cream. Cut slice into two pieces that fit cracker squares. Sandwich each ice cream piece between two crackers, right sides showing. Press together gently. Dip edges into chocolate chip mixture to coat ice cream, pressing lightly in place. Set sandwiches on a platter in the freezer.

Repeat to make 10 more sandwiches. Freeze at least 2 hours or until solid before wrapping individually. Store in the freezer.

Filled S'more Donuts

makes 8

you'll need

- 4 oz. cream cheese, softened (½ C.)
- 1 C. marshmallow creme
- 1 C. powdered sugar
- Vegetable oil for deep-frying
- 1 (8 ct.) tube refrigerated jumbo biscuits (like Grands Homestyle)
- Graham cracker crumbs
- Chopped peanuts

Beat cream cheese, marshmallow creme, and powdered sugar until smooth. Transfer mixture to a piping bag fitted with a large round tip and set aside.

Heat oil in a heavy pot or deep-fryer to 375°. Fry biscuits one at a time for 2 to 3 minutes on each side or until golden brown and cooked through. Set on paper towels to cool.

Insert piping tip into the side of each donut and squeeze filling into center. Frost with Chocolate Icing and sprinkle with crumbs and peanuts.

Chocolate Icing: Place 1¾ C. plus 2 T. powdered sugar in a bowl. Heat ¼ C. butter, 1½ T. unsweetened cocoa powder, and 3 T. cola to a boil. Pour over powdered sugar and whisk until smooth. Spread promptly.

Happy Hour S'moretini

shaken

serves 1

you'll need

Chocolate syrup

Graham cracker crumbs

2 oz. marshmallow vodka

1 oz. chocolate vodka

1 oz. crème de cacao

2 oz. half & half

Fresh strawberry or regular marshmallow

Pour some chocolate syrup into a shallow dish and place crumbs in another dish. Lightly dip the rim of a martini glass in syrup and then gently roll rim in crumbs. Refrigerate until set.

In a cocktail shaker, combine marshmallow vodka, chocolate vodka, crème de cacao, and half & half. Fill with ice and shake well. Strain into prepared glass. Garnish edge of glass with a strawberry or marshmallow. Drizzle with additional syrup, if desired.

makes 20

SUPER S'MORES CUPCAKES

you'll need

½ C. brown sugar

3 T. butter, melted

1¼ C. graham cracker crumbs, divided

1½ C. flour

1½ C. sugar

1 tsp. baking powder

1 tsp. baking soda

¾ C. unsweetened cocoa powder

1 C. milk

½ C. vegetable oil

2 eggs

2 tsp. vanilla

1 (7 oz.) jar marshmallow creme

20 regular marshmallows

20 Kit Kat Minis

to make

Heat oven to 350°. Line 20 muffin cups with paper liners. Mix brown sugar, butter, and ½ cup crumbs; set aside.

Whisk together flour, sugar, baking powder, and baking soda; divide mixture into two bowls (1½ cups each). To one bowl, stir in remaining ¾ cup crumbs; to other bowl, stir in cocoa powder. To each bowl, stir in ½ cup milk, ¼ cup oil, 1 egg, and 1 teaspoon vanilla. Fill cupcake liners ⅓ full with cracker batter; sprinkle with reserved crumbs. Spoon chocolate batter on top until ⅔ full; sprinkle with more crumbs. Bake 15 to 18 minutes. Cool completely.

Spritz a pastry bag with cooking spray and fill with marshmallow creme; pipe filling into top of cupcakes. Broil marshmallows on a sprayed, foil-lined cookie sheet until browned. Cool slightly and set a marshmallow on each cupcake; top with a Kit Kat. Serve promptly.

Razzle Dazzle Delish

Between chocolate graham crackers, layer mini chocolate chips or a milk chocolate candy bar, fresh raspberries, and a toasted marshmallow.

Lemon Lovin'

Open up a lemon sandwich cookie and spread one half with lemon or cherry pie filling and chopped white chocolate. Top with a toasted marshmallow and remaining cookie half.

Nutella-Banana Buzz

Spread Nutella on a graham cracker and add a toasted marshmallow and banana slices. Top with another cracker.

Strawberry Granola Bites

Layer sliced strawberries and a toasted marshmallow between the chocolate sides of two Nature Valley Granola Thins.

Snicker Doodlin'

Spread chocolate frosting on a snicker doodle cookie. Top with a thick slice of red pear, a toasted marshmallow, and another cookie.

serves 10

HOT STUFF MALLOW BRAID

you'll need

1 (8 oz.) tube refrigerated crescent seamless dough sheet

3 T. butter, melted

1 C. coarse graham cracker crumbs

½ C. semi-sweet chocolate chips

¼ C. sliced almonds

¼ C. chocolate toffee bits

⅓ C. sweetened condensed milk, divided

¾ to 1 C. marshmallow creme

2 T. mini chocolate chips

to make

Heat oven to 350°. Coat a rimmed baking sheet with cooking spray. Unroll dough on pan and flatten to 9½ x 13″. Mix butter and crumbs; spread down center third of dough rectangle, stopping 1″ from ends. Sprinkle ½ cup chocolate chips over crumbs. Sprinkle with almonds and toffee bits. Drizzle with all but 2 tablespoons sweetened condensed milk. Spoon marshmallow creme over filling. Make 1″ wide cuts on long sides of dough rectangle to within 1″ of filling.

Fold both dough ends over filling. Alternately fold opposite strips across filling to resemble a braid. Tuck last strips under braid. Brush top with remaining sweetened condensed milk and sprinkle with mini chocolate chips. Bake 18 to 20 minutes or until golden brown. Cool slightly; drizzle with icing.

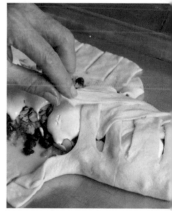

Icing: Whisk together ¾ C. sifted powdered sugar with just enough warm water to make a thin icing.

Éclair Dreams

serves 24

you'll need

- 1 (14.4 oz.) box graham crackers, divided
- 2 (3.4 oz.) pkgs. vanilla instant pudding mix
- 3½ C. plus 6 T. milk, divided
- 1 (12 oz.) tub whipped topping, thawed
- 1 (7 oz.) jar marshmallow creme
- 6 T. butter
- 6 T. unsweetened cocoa powder, sifted
- 1 C. powdered sugar, sifted

Line bottom of a 9 x 13˝ baking pan *(at least 2˝ deep)* with whole crackers, breaking them to fit as needed.

Whisk both pudding mixes into 3½ cups milk until thick and smooth, about 2 minutes. Fold in whipped topping. Spread half the mixture over cracker layer in pan. Microwave marshmallow creme briefly to drizzling consistency; drizzle half over pudding layer. Top with another layer of crackers, pressing down lightly. Spread remaining pudding mixture over crackers and drizzle with remaining marshmallow creme. Layer remaining crackers on top and press lightly.

Microwave butter and remaining 6 tablespoons milk until butter melts. Whisk in cocoa powder and powdered sugar until smooth. Spread over top of dessert. Chill overnight or freeze.

Raspberry Crepes

makes 12

you'll need

- 4 eggs
- 1¼ C. milk
- 1 tsp. vanilla
- Dash of salt
- 2 C. flour
- ¼ C. butter, melted
- **Filling:** chocolate frosting, milk chocolate chips, fresh raspberries, chocolate graham cracker crumbs, mini marshmallows

Whisk eggs with milk, vanilla, salt, and 1 cup water. Gradually whisk in flour until smooth. Add butter and mix well.

Heat a nonstick skillet over medium heat. Pour ¼ to ⅓ cup batter into skillet and rotate to coat bottom of pan with a thin even layer. Cook 1 to 2 minutes or until set and edges start to curl. Flip crepe and remove pan from heat. Spread frosting over half the crepe and sprinkle with chocolate chips. Top with raspberries, crumbs, and marshmallows. Fold crepe in half; cover pan and return to heat just until marshmallows melt. Repeat to make additional crepes. Serve warm with whipped topping, if desired.

Go bananas with this filling instead. Smear hazelnut spread (such as Nutella) over half the crepe, followed by semi-sweet chocolate chips, banana slices, graham cracker crumbs, and mini marshmallows. Mmmm...

oven

Meltaways

makes 48

you'll need

48 chocolate Kisses

⅔ C. butter, softened

1¼ C. sugar

1 tsp. vanilla

2 eggs

1 C. flour

1 C. graham cracker crumbs, divided

½ C. unsweetened cocoa powder

½ tsp. salt

½ tsp. baking soda

Marshmallow creme

Place unwrapped Kisses in the freezer while mixing dough. Beat together butter, sugar, vanilla, and 1 tablespoon water. Add eggs and beat well. In another bowl, mix flour, ½ cup crumbs, cocoa powder, salt, and baking soda; add to sugar mixture and beat until blended. Cover and refrigerate until dough is firm enough to handle, about 2 hours *(or overnight)*.

To bake, heat oven to 350°. Line mini muffin cups with paper liners. Shape dough into 1″ balls and roll in remaining ½ cup crumbs as desired; set in liners. Bake 9 to 10 minutes or until set, but still soft *(don't over-bake)*. Cool in pan for 2 minutes. Put a dab of marshmallow creme in the center of each cookie and bake until puffy, but not brown, about 5 minutes more. Remove from oven and set a Kiss on each cookie. Let cool before removing from pan.

No-Bake Mini Pies

Beat 1 (8 oz.) pkg. softened cream cheese with 1 C. whipped topping, 1 C. powdered sugar, and ½ C. marshmallow creme. Spoon into six mini graham cracker pie crusts; chill.

Bring ⅓ C. heavy cream to a simmer over medium-low heat. Remove from heat; stir in ⅔ C. semi-sweet chocolate chips until melted. Let cool almost completely. Spoon chocolate over pies and top with whipped topping and graham cracker crumbs. Chill until serving.

makes 6

Swirlicious Brownies

Line a 9 x 13˝ baking pan with foil and coat with cooking spray. Using a 9 x 13˝ size fudge brownie mix, prepare batter with egg, oil, and water as directed on box and stir in ⅔ C. semi-sweet chocolate chips. Spread batter in pan.

Microwave ⅔ C. marshmallow creme for 15 seconds and drizzle over batter. Sprinkle with ⅓ C. graham cracker crumbs and swirl through batter with a knife. Bake as directed on box. Let cool. Remove from pan before cutting.

makes 20

Rocky Road Fudge Bars

makes 18

you'll need

- 1½ C. lightly salted whole almonds
- 8 whole graham crackers
- 1 C. marshmallow creme
- 2 C. semi-sweet chocolate chips
- 1 (14 oz.) can sweetened condensed milk

Heat oven to 375°. Spread almonds in a shallow pan and toast in oven for 7 to 10 minutes. Let cool and chop coarsely. Line bottom of a 9 x 13″ baking pan with crackers, breaking them to fit as needed. Bake 7 to 8 minutes or until lightly toasted.

Sprinkle chopped almonds over crackers. Drop spoonfuls of marshmallow creme evenly over the top.

Combine chocolate chips and sweetened condensed milk in a heatproof bowl. Set bowl over a pan of simmering water on the stovetop and stir until melted and smooth. Pour chocolate mixture over marshmallow creme and quickly swirl together with a knife. Chill for 2 hours or until set. Cut into squares. Wrap tightly and store in the refrigerator.

Sweet Spot Scones

makes 8

you'll need

- 2 C. flour
- 1 C. graham cracker crumbs
- 3 T. brown sugar
- 1 T. baking powder
- ¼ tsp. salt
- ½ C. cold butter, cut up
- 1 C. Mallow Bits
- 1 C. semi-sweet or milk chocolate chips
- 1 C. milk, plus more for brushing
- Sugar

Heat oven to 400°. Line a cookie sheet with parchment paper.

Whisk together first five ingredients. Cut in butter until mixture is crumbly. Add Mallow Bits and chocolate chips; toss well. Stir in 1 cup milk, a little at a time, until sticky dough forms. On a floured surface, shape dough into a 9″ round disk, 1″ thick. Brush with milk and sprinkle with sugar. Slice into eight *(or more)* wedges with a pizza cutter and set on cookie sheet, leaving space between them. Bake 14 to 17 minutes or until lightly browned and firm to touch. Cool slightly before drizzling with icing. Serve warm or at room temperature.

Icing: Whisk together ¾ C. sifted powdered sugar with enough heavy cream to make a drizzling consistency.

no
bake

makes 8

PARTY PUDDING SHOTS

you'll need

- 1 (3.9 oz.) box chocolate instant pudding mix
- ¾ C. cold milk
- ½ C. marshmallow vodka
- 1 (8 oz.) tub whipped topping, thawed
- ⅔ C. graham cracker crumbs or crushed honey graham cereal
- Mini marshmallows
- Chocolate candy bar

to make

Whisk together pudding mix and milk until thick and smooth. Slowly whisk in vodka. Fold in whipped topping until well blended. Spoon mixture into a large heavy-duty plastic bag and cut off one corner for piping.

Place about 1 tablespoon crumbs in each of eight small drink or dessert glasses. Pipe pudding mixture over crumbs, filling glasses halfway. Add a layer of marshmallows and pipe more pudding on top. Chill at least 20 minutes.

Before serving, sprinkle with additional marshmallows and garnish with chocolate candy.

Marshmallows may be toasted with a culinary torch.

Hidden Treasure Truffles

makes 28

Heat ⅔ C. heavy cream to a simmer *(don't boil)*. Add 1 C. each semi-sweet and milk chocolate chips and 1 tsp. butter. Let rest until melted, then whisk smooth. Let cool. Refrigerate for 2 hours.

With a melon baller, scoop up a scant tablespoon chocolate mixture and press a mini marshmallow in the center. With damp hands, press chocolate around marshmallow and roll into a smooth ball. Coat with graham cracker crumbs. Repeat until all truffles are made and then roll in crumbs again. Chill for 30 minutes before serving.

Little Bites Granola Balls

makes 24

Combine 1½ C. quick-cooking oats, ¼ C. whole wheat flour, ⅔ C. graham cracker crumbs, and ½ tsp. salt. Stir in ½ C. creamy peanut butter and ½ C. honey until well combined. Add ¼ C. Mallow Bits and ¼ C. milk chocolate chips; mix well. Refrigerate dough for 15 minutes. With hands, form dough into 1˝ balls. Roll in more graham cracker crumbs, if desired.

Pretzel Snackers

Line a cookie sheet with parchment paper and arrange 24 pretzel twists on top. Set one Stacker Mallow and pieces of milk chocolate candy bar on each pretzel. Broil until marshmallows begin to brown and chocolate softens, about 1 minute. Remove from broiler and top with another pretzel. Chill until set.

Melt 1 C. semi-sweet chocolate chips with 1 tsp. shortening, stirring until smooth. Dip pretzel snackers halfway into chocolate and let excess drip off. Set on parchment paper and sprinkle with crushed pretzels while wet. Chill until set.

makes 24

Sweet Waffle Tacos

Microwave a frozen round waffle 10 seconds per side, until warm and pliable. Fold in half and fill with scoops of rocky road ice cream. Top with fudge sauce and Mallow Bits. Add other toppings, like chocolate chips, Teddy Grahams, sliced strawberries, coconut, chopped nuts, whipped cream, and maraschino cherries.

For a party, set up ingredients as a dessert bar.

makes 1

oven

Homemade Graham Crackers

makes 25

you'll need

1½ C. flour
1½ C. graham flour
1 tsp. baking soda
½ tsp. salt
1 C. butter, softened
⅔ C. brown sugar
3 T. honey
Cinnamon-sugar, optional

Whisk together first four ingredients. In another bowl, beat butter, brown sugar, and honey for 2 minutes. Beat in flour mixture and 1 tablespoon water until combined. Work with hands until dough comes together. Set on plastic wrap and press into a 7˝ square; wrap and chill at least 2 hours *(up to 5 days)*.

Before baking, let dough soften at room temperature about 30 minutes. Heat oven to 350°. Line cookie sheets with parchment paper.

Roll out dough on a floured surface to ⅛˝ thickness. Use a square cookie cutter or pizza cutter and 3˝ template to cut dough squares. Place on cookie sheets, leaving space between them. Reroll scraps to cut more.

Pierce cracker tops with a fork and sprinkle with cinnamon-sugar, if desired. Bake 14 to 17 minutes, until deep golden brown and just firm to touch. Cool on pans for 1 minute before removing to cooling rack to crisp up.

Homemade Marshmallows

makes 96 cubes

you'll need

Powdered sugar

2 T. plus 2½ tsp. unflavored gelatin *(3½ (.25 oz.) env.)*

2 C. sugar

½ C. light corn syrup

¼ tsp. salt

2 egg whites, at room temperature

1 T. clear vanilla

Coat a 9 x 13″ baking pan with vegetable oil; dust well with powdered sugar. Sprinkle gelatin over ½ cup cold water in a large bowl and let soften.

In a heavy saucepan, mix sugar, corn syrup, salt, and ½ cup water; cook over low heat, stirring until sugar dissolves. Bring to a boil over medium heat without stirring until a candy thermometer reaches 240°, about 12 minutes. Pour hot mixture over softened gelatin and stir to dissolve. Beat at high speed until thick, white, and nearly tripled in volume, 6 to 10 minutes. *(If mixer slows, turn it off promptly.)*

In a clean bowl, beat egg whites to stiff peaks. Stir whites and vanilla into sugar mixture. Spread in pan and sift ¼ cup powdered sugar over the top. Chill until firm, at least 3 hours *(up to 24 hours).*

Loosen marshmallow from pan with a knife and flip onto a cutting board, easing it out with hands. Cut into 1″ cubes with oiled pizza cutter. Roll in powdered sugar and shake off excess. Store up to 1 week in an airtight container.

INDEX